American Hero Day

by Alice Cary

Illustrated by Barbara Kiwak

PEARSON

Glenview, Illinois • Boston, Massachusetts • Chandler, Arizona
Upper Saddle River, New Jersey

Mr. Brown's second graders were getting ready for American Hero Day. They were making masks of their favorite American heroes.

Suddenly, a cat ran inside the school and stepped in paint. It stepped all over the children's work. It got paint on many of the children's masks. What a disaster!

2

"What can we do?" asked Jin. "Our families are coming to see the masks tonight! Now some of the masks are ruined!"

"We can paint new masks," Mary said.

"We can't paint new masks. There isn't enough time," said Mr. Brown.

"I have an idea," said Carlos. "Do
you remember our visit to Baker School?
They had an American Hero Day too.
Maybe we can borrow their masks."

"That's a great idea!" said Mr. Brown.

Mr. Brown called Mrs. Clay at Baker School.

"May we borrow some of your masks for our American Hero Day?" he asked.

"Of course you can borrow our masks!" Mrs. Clay said. She soon came with many masks.

"Mrs. Clay is our hero!" cried Mary.

The parents came to the school. Everyone was excited.

Then the show began. The second graders came on stage. Some had their own masks. Some had masks from Baker School.

"I'm Sally Ride," Mary said. "I was the first American woman in space."

"I'm George Washington," Greg said. "I was the first President."

"I'm Abraham Lincoln," Thomas said. "I helped all Americans to be free."

The show was a big success. Everyone
clapped for the American heroes.
Everyone clapped for the second
graders.

Then Mr. Brown said, "Today our
show was almost ruined. But Carlos
had a super idea. Carlos was our hero
today!"